GW00601307

# KING ST.

## Set Three
## BOOK 6

# Shane Wants a Girlfriend

NEWHAM LIBRARIES

90800101058182

*Shane Wants a Girlfriend*
King Street: Readers Set Three - Book 6
Copyright © Iris Nunn 2014

Text: Iris Nunn
Editor: June Lewis

Published in 2014 by Gatehouse Media Limited

ISBN: 978-1-84231-131-8

*British Library Cataloguing-in-Publication Data:*
A catalogue record for this book is available from the British Library

No part of this publication may be reproduced in any form or by any means, electronic, mechanical, photocopying, recording or otherwise, without the prior written consent of the publishers.

Shane is twenty.

He works in the pub.
He can drive.
He drives an old car.
He can play the drums.

He is a nice lad,
but he is not happy.

Shane wants a lot of things.
He wants a better car.
He wants a better job.
He wants a girlfriend.

He thinks,
"If I had a better car,
I might get a girlfriend.
If I had a better job,
I might get a girlfriend."

His sister, Meg, says,
"If you talk to girls,
you might get a girlfriend!"

Shane is shy.

He can talk to other lads,
but he can't talk to girls.

He can talk to his sister,
but he can't talk to other girls.

One day he was working on his car.
He was washing his car
outside his house.
His mate, Mike,
came down the street.

"I'll have a word with Mike,"
said Shane to himself.

"Mike, you have a girlfriend.
I want a girlfriend,
but I just can't talk to girls.
Tell me what to say."

Mike said,
"Ask her to go for a walk."

"Where would we walk to?"
said Shane.

"Well, ask her to go
to see a film."

"What film?" said Shane.

"I give up!" said Mike.

That evening,
Shane was washing glasses in the pub.
He said to himself,
"I'll have a word with Brenda.
I can talk to Brenda."

"Brenda, I want a girlfriend,
but I can't talk to girls.
Can you tell me what to say?"

Brenda said,
"You can ask a girl about herself.
You can ask a girl about her family.
You can ask a girl what she likes."

Shane said to himself,
"I will try that."

On Sunday his sister, Meg,
was going out with her friend, Kelly.

Kelly rang Meg up.
Shane picked up the phone.

"Hello, Kelly. How are you?"
he said.

Kelly was a bit surprised.
Usually Shane said,
"I'll get Meg for you,"
and that was all.

Kelly was so surprised she said,
"I've got a job,
a Saturday job."

"Good for you," said Shane.
He was even surprising himself!

When Kelly came to pick up Meg,
Shane was there at the door.
"Tell me about your job,"
he said.

Well, the next time Kelly came
to the house, Shane asked her
if she would like to see a film.

"We can all go together," he said.
"Meg, me and you!"

That was the start.
Shane could talk to girls now.
He liked Kelly
and she liked him!

Very soon they were going out
together,
sometimes with Meg,
sometimes without.

GW00601306

# KING ST.

### Set Four
### THE FIRE

# Ros's Story

NEWHAM LIBRARIES

90800101057467

*Ros's Story*
King Street: Readers Set Four: The Fire
Copyright © Iris Nunn 2014

Text: Iris Nunn
Editor: June Lewis

Published in 2014 by Gatehouse Media Limited

ISBN: 978-1-84231-140-0

*British Library Cataloguing-in-Publication Data:*
A catalogue record for this book is available from the British Library

No part of this publication may be reproduced in any form or by any means, electronic, mechanical, photocopying, recording or otherwise, without the prior written consent of the publishers.

It was hot.

It was dry.

It was ten to nine in the morning.

It was Saturday morning.

It was the morning of August
the tenth.

I was ready for work
because I help in the corner shop
on Saturdays.

I went down the street to the corner
only to find the shop was shut!

Now, Mrs T opens the shop
at 8.30 a.m. as a rule,
but today it was shut.

I knocked on the door.
There was no reply.

I was about to go when, just then,
Mrs T opened the door.
She was in her slippers
and dressing gown.

"Oh Ros! I've been up all night.
We've had a fire.
It was in Frank's flat.
Frank's in hospital.
Come in and have a look."

I went into the shop.
There was a funny smell.
It was the smell of burning.
I went upstairs.
The flat door was open.
It was all smashed.

Inside, everything was black.
Frank's armchair was black.
The curtains were black.
The bed was black.
There was a hole in the carpet
and all the bedding was ruined.
It was a mess.

"We've had the fire brigade,
the police and the ambulance.
Luckily we had Sid round.
He was clearing up in the pub
and he smelt the smoke
through an open window.
He came round at once to help us.
He broke the door down.
I must go and see how Frank is
and call the insurance.
Oh, what a mess!"

"How did it happen?"
I asked Mrs T.

"It was a cigarette, Ros,
and to think I sold them to him!
I've never liked Frank smoking
in his room."

So on Saturday we kept the shop shut
and I helped Mrs T with the cleaning.
There was a lot to do.

That evening, we both went
to see Frank in hospital.